In the fall, we pick pum[pkins that have]
grown big and round a[...]

Pumpkins grow in a pumpkin patch.

In the summer, the pumpkin patch is empty. The farmer must get his field ready for planting.

Now it's time to plant the seeds.

The farmer gives the pumpkin patch lots of water to help the seeds grow.

Then the pumpkin plant grows big leaves and thick vines.

Soon yellow flowers start to bloom.

A pumpkin starts to form beneath the flower. Can you see the pumpkin starting to grow?

Young pumpkins are green.

They grow bigger and bigger,

and then they turn orange!

Some pumpkins grow very big.

Some pumpkins stay very small.

And some pumpkins are just right for making jack-o'-lanterns!

Which pumpkin would you pick?